The Scribblers
of Scumbagg School

Other brilliant books are:

Fizzy Hits the Headlines
MICHAEL COLEMAN

Potion Commotion
JONATHAN ALLEN

B.I.G. Trouble
JONATHAN ALLEN

Tanya the Chicken
SONIA HOLLEYMAN

THE SCRIBBLERS OF SCUMBAGG SCHOOL

Wes Magee

ILLUSTRATIONS BY *Tony Blundell*

ORCHARD BOOKS

ORCHARD BOOKS
96 Leonard Street, London EC2A 4RH
Orchard Books Australia
14 Mars Road, Lane Cove, NSW 2066
First published in Great Britain 1993
First paperback publication 1995
Text © Wes Magee 1993
Illustrations © Tony Blundell 1993

The right of Wes Magee to be identified as the author and Tony Blundell as the illustrator of this work has been asserted by them in accordance with the Copyright, Designs and Patents Act, 1988.
A CIP catalogue record for this book is available from the British Library.

ISBN 1 85213 486 0 (Hardback)

Printed in Great Britain by Bookcraft (Bath) Ltd.

THE TIMETABLE

8.45 a.m.	On Monday Morning
8.55 a.m.	In the Staffroom
9.00 a.m.	Class 2
9.15 a.m.	The First Lesson
10.30 a.m.	Playtime
11.00 a.m.	Mrs Dreggs and the Boiler House Beast
11.10 a.m.	The Secret Notes of Class 2
11.45 a.m.	An Interview
12.00 noon	Lunchtime
12.45 p.m.	The Dinner Hour Rap
1.15 p.m.	The Art Lesson (Class 2)
2.30 p.m.	The Out-of-date Valentine's Day Card
3.00 p.m.	A Letter for N.O. Funear, Headmonster
3.30 p.m.	The End of the School Day

8.45 a.m.

On Monday Morning

It was a Monday morning in March. The weather was bitterly cold. Winter's frozen fingers still gripped the town. And overnight snow had fallen. This morning a white sheet of snow covered the playground at Scumbagg School.

In ones,
 twos,
  threes,
   fours,
    fives
    and
     sixes the pupils began to arrive. Within seconds they were all hard at work – playing in the snow.

They were
laughing and leaping
and slipping and sliding,
   and reeling and rolling
   and piggy-back riding,
shrieking and squealing
and crying and calling,
   jostling and jumping
   and fooling and falling,
grunting and groaning
and bashing and bawling,

  and
    all of them
     all of them
    ALL
     were
      snowballing!

Then the bell rang.

It was eight forty-five.

"You lot! Inside!" shouted Mrs Squash. "Look alive!"

Ninety-nine excited (and wet) children shambled slowly into Scumbagg School. Mrs Squash, the teacher on duty, tried to chase them along.

Bags
were dumped.
Mike
got thumped.
In the cloakroom
voices
boomed.
Girls
shoved boys.
Wow!
What noise!
Mrs Squash
fussed and
fumed.

And slowly, slowly, *slowly* the pupils went down the long corridor to their classrooms. Mrs Squash wobbled towards the staffroom.

8.55 a.m.

In the Staffroom

"They're in!" bellowed Mrs Squash as she barged her way into the staffroom.

Little Miss Duff stopped knitting and looked over her half-specs.

Tall Mr Soap yawned in the easy chair.

"Come on, you two, out of those chairs," said Mrs Squash. "They're in!"

"Baloney!" said Mr Soap. He stretched out his long legs, and yawned again.

Mrs Squash gulped down a mug of lukewarm tea, then wiped her mouth on the back of her hand. "Time we were in our classrooms," she said. "Come on, before the Headmaster finds us hiding here."

"Okay, okay," said Mr Soap. He stood up. He was very tall.

Miss Duff stood up. She was very little.

She stuffed her knitting into a plastic bag.

"After you, ladies," said Mr Soap, and he ushered them out of the staffroom.

The three teachers walked in line down the long corridor – wobbly Mrs Squash, little Miss Duff, and tall Mr Soap.

As they reached the classrooms they were met by the raucous noise of children's voices.

"Here we go," muttered Mr Soap. "Here we go!"

Mrs. Squash (Class 1)

Mrs. Cynthia Squash teaches Class 1. She is large and amazingly wobbly. She gets really mad when the girls fall out and go all catty and squabbly. The big skirt she wears hangs down to the floor and hides knees that are horribly knobbly.

Mr. Soap (Class 2)

Mr. Soap's name is Joe.
He is tall.
He is bald.
He is bony.
A spiky black beard
sprouts from his chin
and he's always saying
'Baloney!'

Class 2 is his mob,
thirty-two rowdy kids,
and all of them call him
'Old Groany!'

old groany →

Miss Duff (Class 3)

Little Miss Duff
　(first name—Daffodil)
is short-sighted.
Her age could be eighty.
She teaches class 3,
　cluck-clucks like a hen,
and likes to be friendly
　and matey.
Her squeaky-squeak voice
gets on everyone's nerves
—it sounds so grindy
　and gratey.

P.S. The Headmaster
has yet to arrive.
　Be patient.
Just wait for a while.
But when he appears
take note of his name
and beware of his
　Dracula smile.

9.00 a.m.

Class 2

"Hhrrmmmm!" Mr Soap stood in the doorway and cleared his throat. "Hhrrmmmm!" The children in Class 2 scuttled to their places.

Chairs banged.

Chairs scraped.

Voices died down.

All eyes were fixed on 'Old Groany'.

"That's more like it," said Mr Soap. He strode to his desk, sat down, tugged at his spiky black beard, and threw open the register.

"Yes, Mr Soap!" the children shouted as he called their names.

"Here, Mr Soap!"

"Yes, Mr Soap!"

And some of the names belonged to:

KATRINA KIZZKURLL
A tiny girl
with a huge shock
of red hair.

DICK FISH
A big boy
with a gaping mouth
and vacant stare.

GILLIAN GILES
Hardest worker
and best writer
in Scumbagg School.

MIKE ELANGELO
He's got
goofy teeth
but thinks he's cool.

TRACEY TRUMPET
A blondie
who wears
Santa Claus socks.

ROBERT R. ROBERTS
The 'Professor';
a big-head
and a brain-box ...

... and lots more.
In total, thirty-two.

Some like me
and a few like you.
Cheeky ones,
cheery ones,
and those who haven't a clue.
Some are mopes,
some are dopes,
and they all live together
in 'Old Groany' Soap's.

That's Class 2.

9.15 a.m.

The First Lesson

"Hhrrmmmm! Time to work," said Mr Soap.

"What are we going to do?" asked tiny Katrina Kizzkurll.

"Is it easy?" asked big Dick Fish.

"Is it hard?" asked Tracey Trumpet.

"Not *too* easy, I hope," said 'Professor' Robert R. Roberts.

"Quiet! No more questions," said Mr Soap. He walked up and down in front of the blackboard. He jiggled a stick of white chalk in his long, bony fingers.

The children watched.

Someone sniffed. Someone coughed.

Someone hissed.

Mike Elangelo whistled through his goofy teeth.

At last Mr Soap spoke. "This morning you are going to write."

"Write what?" asked Dick Fish.

"How many pages?" asked Mike Elangelo.

Mr Soap ignored the questions. He wrote on the blackboard:

"That's the title," said Mr Soap. He smacked his hands and a little cloud of dust rose into the air.

"Writing books opennnnn," he continued. "Pens at the readyyyyy. Now, get on with it, and no baloney!"

There was a bit of mumbling.

There was a bit of fumbling.

There was a bit of grumbling, and someone's tummy was hunger-rumbling.

But one after another the children of Class 2 settled down to write. A silence descended …

WHAT I DID AT THE WEEKEND
by Dick Fish.

On Saturday morning
I played football
for the Beavers
down the rec.
I was striker.
The other team
was Moss Lane Stars.
Our trainer, Mr Coole,
kept on at me.
'Fish! You big kipper!'
he shouted.
'Stop playing
the fool!'

That night
I had a whole tin
of baked-beans-with-eight-sausages
for my supper.
It was ace!
Then our dog, Snapper,
chewed my dad's slipper
and left bits
all over
the place.

On Sunday
my friend
Kevin Kickapoo
came round to play.
We broke a vase
and stuck it together
with glue.
That's all I did
at the weekend.

My mum says I'm driving her right round the bend.

The End.

10.30 a.m.

Playtime!

The bell rang. Playtime! Playtime – in the snow!

"Hhrrmmmm," said Mr Soap. "Stop writing. I hope you've written good reports."

"I have," said 'Professor' Robert R. Roberts.

Everyone turned and stared at him.

"Gillian Giles," said Mr Soap, "collect the books. The rest of you – out to play."

The tall teacher was swept aside as a tidal wave of children burst through the door. The long corridor was shrill with voices as pupils from Mrs Squash's, Miss Duff's and Mr Soap's classes headed for the playground.

But they skidded to a halt outside the Headmaster's room. Miss Mess, the school secretary, was pinning a notice on the Red Board.

"This is for you lot," Miss Mess told the children.

Everyone scrummed round,
stretching,
straining,
and neck-craning
to read the notice.

Headmaster:

N.O.Funear, BA(d)

    Scumbagg School,

    Slow Lane,

    NUTTERSALL,

    Burks. IOU 50P

TO THE PUPILS OF SCUMBAGG SCHOOL

A new week starts today and there are new rules ... for play.

When there is SNOW
the word you must learn
is ... NO!

NO ice slides

NO snowballing

NO fighting

NO falling

DON'T chase

DON'T throw snow in
someone's face.

Know
that accidents in snow

```
can be

appalling.

When there is SNOW

the word you must learn

is ... NO!

    Signed: N.O.Funear
                (Headmaster)
```

After reading the notice the children groaned. Mr Soap's pupils were the first to grumble.

"Our headmaster's a wrecker!" said tiny Katrina Kizzkurll.

"He's a right old misery guts!" said big Dick Fish.

"He won't let us play in the snow!" said Mike Elangelo.

"Actually, he's an interfering busy-body, a negative Nosy Parker, and an utter, *utter* ultracrepidarian ... if you really want to know!"

The children gaped.

The children stared.

Who had spoken?

'Professor' Robert R. Roberts, of course. He'd received *The Concise Oxford Dictionary (New Edition)* for his birthday, and he'd read the 1,454 pages ... every one.

But then
with a slow shuffling
with some nose snuffling
and a bit of scuffling
the children went to the playground,
sighing ...

Mrs Squash, who was on duty in the playground, stamped her frozen feet. She warmed her hands around a mug of steaming tea.

"Don't forget the Headmaster's order," she told the children. "No snowballing."

The children looked glum.

Some of the boys played football but the playground was too skiddy and slippery. Someone kicked the ball extra hard and it landed on top of the P.E. shed. Dick Fish climbed up to retrieve it.

"Get down!" shouted Mrs Squash. "You're breaking a school rule! I'll report you to the Headmaster!"

Dick Fish threw the football off the roof, and then he climbed down, glaring at Mrs Squash.

When the bell rang the children trooped back into school. They were surprised (very) to discover that someone (who?) had removed the Headmaster's notice from the Red Board. A new notice had been pinned up in its place. The notice was neatly handwritten in green ink on a sheet of file paper.

> To the pupils of Scumbag School
>
> Today
> the word you must learn is... YES!
>
> YES,
> you can throw snowballs.
> YES,

you can build snowmen,
  make ice slides,
    put up an igloo.
YES
 go ahead!
Make a mess!

Why not
scrawl a snow poem on the toilet wall?
Why not
do a snow dance in the hall?
Why not
race down the corridor,
sing,
and shout?
Be a menace!
Be a lout!

Today
the word you must learn is... YES!

> Go on,
> have a blow.
> Enjoy yourself in the snow.
> Do MORE
> not less.
> The word you must learn is...YES!
>
> Signed: O.K. Doitall
> (Headmonster)

"Who wrote it?"
the children asked. "Who?"

"Robert R. Roberts,
was it you?"

The 'Professor' shook his head.
"But I recognise the handwriting," he said.
He gave one of his clever-clogs smiles.
"It's by the best writer in Scumbagg School."

And all the children chorused,
   "Gillian Giles!"

All the pupils
thought Gillian's note was really cool.
It made Headmaster Funear
look like a soppy old fool.

11.00 a.m.

Mrs Dreggs and the Boiler House Beast

Mrs Dreggs, Scumbagg School Caretaker, placed a note on the Headmaster's desk. She had written it on a sheet torn from the *Page-a-Day Joke Diary (1984)* she kept in her small broom-filled room. Mrs Eggy-Dreggy (as the children called her) had folded the note and written on the front:

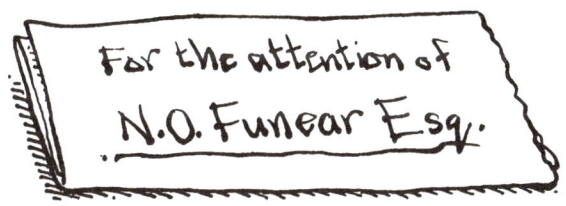

The Headmaster found the note when he returned from seeing Mrs Squash. She had reported (yet again!) that dreadful Dick Fish boy. Mr Funear would have to see him.

And, to make matters worse, Miss Mess told him that someone had removed his notice from the Red Board. What cheek! And now, the last straw, there was a note – *another* note – from Mrs Dreggs.

N.O. Funear permitted himself the ghost of a Dracula smile.

THE PAGE-A-DAY JOKE DIARY FOR 1984

Thursday 5th February

'What did the Mummy Ghost say to the little ghost?

✫ ✫ ✫ ✫ ✫ ✫ ✫ ✫ ✫ ✫

'Don't spook until you are spoken to!'
(from a Hong Kong Christmas cracker)

Headmaster,
   there's something nasty, right,
      something scary
         in my Boiler-House.
I heard a squeak,
   a <u>loud</u> squeak.
      Was it, I asked myself,
         a <u>mouse</u>?
Then, I was sweeping up, right,
sweeping this way and that,
when I heard it again,
the squeak.
Only louder this time.
Was it, I asked myself,
   a <u>rat</u>?
I pushed my broom, right,
under Boilers One and Two.
      Nothing there.

Nothing, except the concrete floor.
But the squeaking goes on, and on, and <u>on</u>, much louder than b before.
And then I saw something!
Oh me!
Oh my!
And I'll tell you what I saw!

Behind the Boilers
    (One and Two, right)
in the dust,
in the dark
I saw...
    a terrible sight.
    A <u>THING</u>...

...with three bloodshot eyes
and hairy arms.
What a scare!
What a fright!

Headmaster,
there's a beast in the Boiler House!
Right!
From your umble servant,
Mrs. T.H.E. Dreggs
(Caretaker)

Headmaster Funear
slumped back in his chair.
He was losing his mind.
He was losing his hair.
   Mrs Dreggs
   Mrs Dreggs
she was driving him mad.
She'd got Beasts on the brain,
    really bad
    really bad.
At least once a week
she wrote him a note

about horrors, or werewolves,
or ghosts "at her throat".
   Mrs Dreggs
   Mrs Dreggs
she was driving him mad.
She'd got Beasts on the brain,
   really bad
   really bad.

What *would* she see next?
Vampire, gremlin or ghoul?
High time, the Head thought,
that she left Scumbagg School.
   Mrs Dreggs
   Mrs Dreggs
she was driving him mad.
She'd got Beasts on the brain,
   really bad
   really bad.

Mr Funear reached for a memo pad. Wearily he took a pen from his jacket pocket and began to write …

Memo: to Mrs. T.H.E. Dreggs

From: The Headmaster

Thank you
for your note.
I am sorry
you had such a bad fright.
Three bloodshot eyes this time!
My, my,
what a truly terrible
sight.
I think
it's about time
you resigned.
Right.
<u>N.O.F.</u>

11.10 a.m.

The Secret Notes of Class 2

While Headmaster Funear was dealing with Mrs Dreggs's latest complaint, Mr Soap was setting Class 2 their work.

"This will keep you busy until lunch-time," he announced. And he wrote on the blackboard:

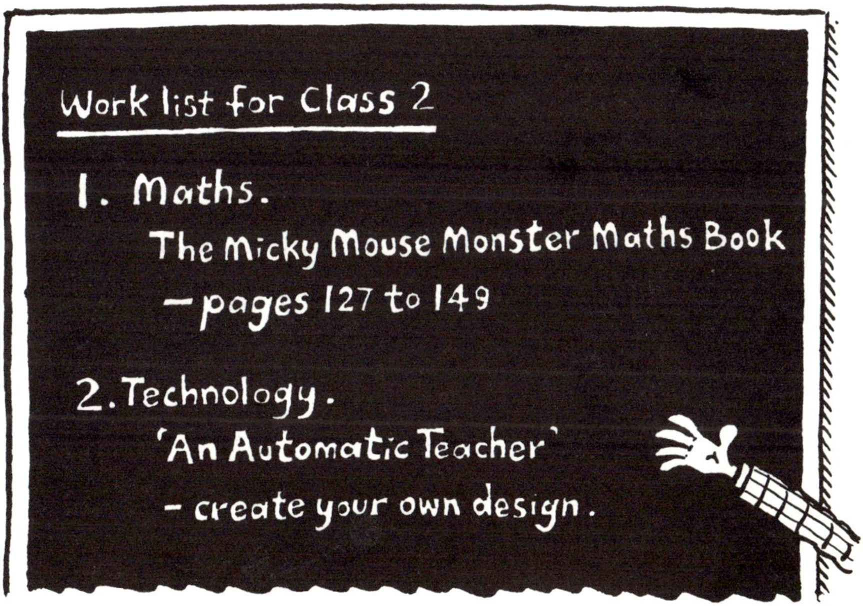

Work list for Class 2

1. Maths.
   The Micky Mouse Monster Maths Book
   — pages 127 to 149

2. Technology.
   'An Automatic Teacher'
   — create your own design.

> 3. History.
> Read Chapter 6. and make notes
> – 'Victorian children working down a mine.

"There," said Mr Soap, "and now I'm going to mark your 'Weekend' reports. So get working! Now!"

The children started their work, but it wasn't long before notes were being secretly passed from one pupil to another.

Heather Heavirain was another pupil in Mr Soap's class. She had a crush on Dick Fish. She got her best friend, Tracey Trumpet (who could write really well) to send Dick a secret letter. Tracey carefully tore a sheet of paper from her Rough Notes book, and wrote:

> To dear dishy Dick,
> Can
> you come to my party?
> It's tomorrow night.
> Heather Beavirain
> wants to meet you there.
> All right?
>
> Keep this invitation
> Don't dump it.
>
> Best wishes from
> Tracey Trumpet
> (and Heather!) X

Dick was not pleased to receive Tracey's note. He screwed it up and dropped it on the floor. In his pocket he found a Swimming Note that he hadn't taken home. On the back of the slip he scribbled a reply to Tracey – and Heather:

> To Tracey Trumpet.
> Look,
> leave it out, will you!
> I <u>hate</u> parties!
> And I <u>don't</u> like
> <u>Heather Heavirain</u>.
> All girls are hopeless
> but she is a real
> pain.
> from Dick Fish.
> P.S. Don't write to me again!

Mike Elangelo liked tiny Katrina Kizzkurll. In fact he quite fancied her. In fact he was in love with her.

On the last page of his Maths work book Mike wrote a poem for Katrina – and he secretly passed it to her under the table.

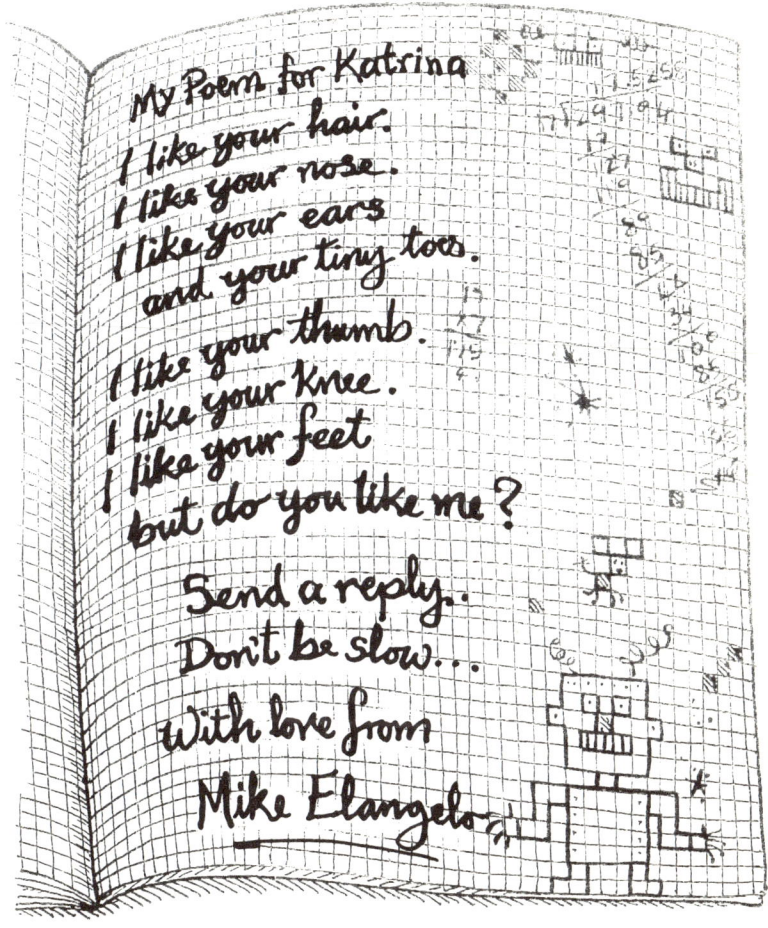

Katrina Kizzkurll was tiny, but she had a big fiery temper. She was determined to put Mike Elangelo firmly in his place. On a paper tissue she drew a picture of herself. Then she gave herself a speech bubble, and threw it across to Mike.

Mickey Hamsterhead was a quiet boy in Mr Soap's class. He sat next to Dalinda Parrotstick. He wrote her a note on a paper towel he'd taken from the boys' washroom:

> Dearest Dalinda,
> Meet me at lunchtime behind the P.E shed. And don't tell anyone or you're dead!
>
> With love from
> Mickey Hamsterhead

Mickey's note made Dalinda Parrotstick cross. She threw it into Mr Soap's bin, then returned to her place and wrote a reply on an old sheet of tracing paper:

> Mickey,
> you nit!
> Are you a Norman,
> or just a twit?
>
> Meet you?
> No way!
> You're thick
> as a house brick.
>
> You get on my wick!
>
> Get lost!
>
> Dalinda Parrotstick.

Mr Soap finished marking the 'Weekend' reports. He walked around the classroom, handing back the children's writing books.

He found a screwed-up ball of paper on the floor, and then another. They were the 'secret' notes.

"What's all this?" Mr Soap asked Dick Fish.

"I dunno," mumbled Dick Fish.

"Baloney!" said Mr Soap, and he tugged at his spiky black beard.

He strode to the blackboard, rubbed off the work list, and wrote:

11.45 a.m.

An Interview

Just before lunchtime Miss Mess walked into Mr Soap's classroom and handed him a note.

"It's from the Headmaster," she said.

Mr Soap read the note. He frowned.

"Dick Fish," he said sternly, "the Headmaster wants to see you – now."

Dick Fish followed Miss Mess down the long corridor. Her high heels click-click-clicked.

"What's he want me for?" asked Dick glumly.

"Wait and see," said Miss Mess, "wait and see."

At the Headmaster's room Miss Mess knocked, and then opened the door.

"Dick Fish to see you, Headmaster," she said, and firmly pushed the big boy inside.

The Headmaster glanced up, and gave one of his Dracula smiles ...

"Ah, Fish," he said, "Mrs Squash has reported you, once more!"
(Dick Fish stared at the carpet on the floor.)
"She caught you climbing on the roof of the P.E. shed. Tut! Tut!"
(Dick Fish kept his big mouth firmly shut.)
"I think I'll have to write and tell your father and mother."
(Dick Fish shifted from one foot to the other.)
"You've broken a school rule. It's two hundred lines for you, my lad."
(Dick Fish was feeling angry, cross, and mad.)

"Write them at lunchtime. Make sure you finish them today!"

(Dick Fish turned,
and slowly
walked
away.)

... and already he was planning his revenge ...

12.00 NOON

Lunchtime

At 12.00 noon the bell rang. The children raced to the hall where tables had been set up by the dinner ladies.

The teachers headed for the staffroom.

Mrs Squash gulped yet another mug of tea.

Mr Soap slumped in his easy chair.

Little Miss Duff fixed her half-specs on the end of her nose and took out her knitting.

Outside, the sun had appeared. The snow was rapidly melting. Mrs Dreggs was sweeping the slush to one side of the playground, but every twenty seconds she glanced nervously at the Boiler House door.

Back in the hall the children were tucking into their dinner. Naturally, things were not totally peaceful. The dinner ladies prowled up and down, up and down …

Dinner ladies on the prowl.
 HERE THEY COME!
  WATCH OUT!
Dinner ladies on the prowl.
How they screech and shout!

Robert chews cold cabbage,
Clara's chomping chips,
Sue slurps up spaghetti,
Tracey's spitting pips.

Gill has left her lettuce,
Gaz flicks bits of pie,
Dick Fish peels an orange
– squirts juice in his eye.

Dinner ladies on the prowl.
 HERE THEY COME!
  WATCH OUT!
Dinner ladies on the prowl.
How they screech and shout!

Tim has turtle pizza,
Mickey drains a Coke,
Heather's sarnies make her
splutter, cough, and choke.

Mike hates mashed potato,
Kat has creamy cheese,
Matthew has a bad cold
– gives a monster sneeze.

Dinner ladies on the prowl.
  HERE THEY COME!
  WATCH OUT!
Dinner ladies on the prowl.
How they screech and shout!

Andy drops his lunch box
– food across the floor!
Suddenly the cook bawls,
"Seconds! Who wants more?"

Rushing, pushing children.
"Get in line! Be quick!"
Poor Dalinda whimpers,
"Miss, I'm feeling sick!".

Dinner ladies on the prowl.
HERE THEY COME!
WATCH OUT!
Dinner ladies on the prowl.
How they screech and shout!

But, at last, at long last
everyone had finished
and they all went out to play.
But, to their disappointment,
the snow had all melted away.

The children stood around, wondering what to do. Then some girls and boys started a chant:

Din-ner Ladies! (CLAP CLAP CLAP)
Din-ner Ladies! (CLAP CLAP CLAP)
    Ladies! (CLAP)
    Ladies! (CLAP)
Din-ner Ladies! (CLAP CLAP CLAP)

Yes, the children played out ... except Dick Fish. He (do you remember?) had two hundred lines to write for Headmaster Funear. With a scowl on his face Dick settled down in the Library and started:

> I must not climb on top of the P.E. shed.
> I must not climb on top of the P.E. shed.
> I mist nut climb on top of the P.E. Shed.
> I mist not clumb on tip of the P.E. shmd.

He was so busy writing that he hardly noticed the four girls who entered the Library ...

12.45 p.m.

The Dinner Hour Rap

The four girls were Gillian Giles, Katrina Kizzkurll, Tracey Trumpet and Dalinda Parrotstick. They were all from Class 2.

"It's Dick Fish," said Gillian Giles. "What are you doing?"

"Lines," said Dick, "Two hundred lines for the Headmonster."

"Naughty boy," said Katrina Kizzkurll.

The girls laughed.

"And what are you lot here for?" asked Dick.

"We're writing a Rap," said Gillian. "So keep quiet and let us get on with it."

The girls sat down. Gillian, the best writer in Scumbagg School, did all the work. When the Rap was finished the girls went to the school office and asked Miss Mess to make some copies.

"How many?" asked Miss Mess.

"Four copies," said Tracey Trumpet, "so we can have one each."

Miss Mess tapped the '4' button on the photo-copying machine. Unfortunately her finger touched the button twice – and forty-four copies were printed!

The girls were delighted. They ran onto the playground and handed out the sheets. Soon dozens of children were chanting the Dinner Hour Rap.

The Dinner Hour Rap

written by Gillian, Katrina, Tracey
and Dalinda

We've
been
working for the teachers
and eating in the hall
working in the classrooms
- it hasn't been a ball!
But
get a little hip
and give your thighs a slap
then take a little skip
and give your hands a clap
and let yourself go
with the
Dinner
Hour
Rap!

We've
been
writing in our notebooks
and writing on the floor
writing in the toilets
~ who's written on the door?
But
get a little hip
and give your thighs a slap
then take a little skip
and give your hands a clap
and let yourself go
with the
Dinner
Hour
Rap!

We've
been
told off by the teachers
the Head has made us blue
the dinners are disgusting
— the custard tastes like glue
    But
    get a little hip
    and give your thighs a slap
    then take a little skip
    and give your hands a clap
    and let yourself go
    with the
Dinner
Hour
Rap!

We've
been
in this place all morning
and if we had our way
we'd sack the rotten teachers
and close the school today!
So
get a little hip
and give your thighs a slap
then take a little skip
and give your hands a clap
and let yourself go
with the
Dinner
Hour
Rap!
YEAH!

1.15 p.m.

The Art Lesson (Class 2)

Mr Soap organised the weekly painting lesson. He hated it. Something *always* went wrong. But the Headmaster insisted that it was on the timetable.

All the children wore art shirts. These helped to keep their clothes clean. Some of the shirts had extra long sleeves, some were too big, some were ripped, and all were plastered with dried paint. The pupils of Class 2 looked a dreadful sight.

"Where's Dick Fish?" asked Mr Soap.

"Finishing his lines in the Library," said Gillian Giles.

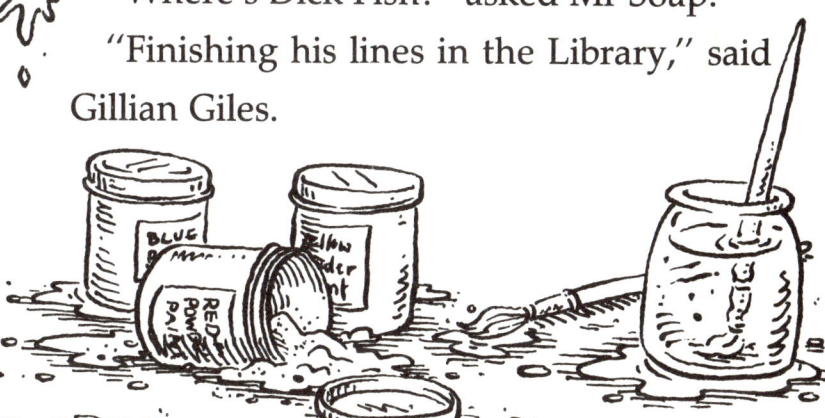

Mr Soap frowned, but felt secretly relieved. That big boy always caused trouble during the art lesson.

But even without Dick Fish it wasn't long before disaster struck.

Tracey Trumpet
spilled water
and a lake formed on the floor.

Robert R. Roberts
left blue fingerprints
across the classroom door.

Gillian Giles
blobbed paint
all over her wooden chair

Mike Elangelo
(somehow) paint-shampooed
his hair.

Katrina Kizzkurll
dabbed green spots
on her chin and nose.

Kevin Kickapoo
took off his shoes
and multi-coloured his toes.

And Dalinda Parrotstick
(for the second time that day)
felt
sick.

Poor 'Old Groany' Soap
wished he was home
tucked up in bed.
Class 2 made him feel like
tearing his hair
out of his head.

(but he couldn't,
could he,
because he was bald!)

"Right," said Mr Soap, "art lesson over! Clear away!"

And at that very moment who should walk into the classroom but – Dick Fish.

Mr Soap turned on him.

"Fish," he stormed, "have you finished those two hundred lines?"

"Yes, I have," said Dick.

"Well, where are they?"

"Gave'm to Miss Mess," said the big boy. "And she'll give'm to the Head-monster."

"The *who*?" asked Mr Soap.

"The Headmaster," said Dick quickly.

And Dick Fish went to his place. But there was a secretive grin on his face. What had he been up to?

2.30 p.m.

The Out-of-date Valentine's Day Card

Gillian Giles discovered a red envelope in her work tray. On the front there was a big love heart with an arrow through the middle.

At one end of the arrow were the initials 'G.G.'

At the other end a '?'

Gillian tore open the red envelope and found a Valentine's Day card inside.

To darling Gillian,
I am sorry
this Valentine
is a month late!

But.
Will you go out with me
and be my
date?   x x x
Meet me
at half-past three
down by the school gate.
That's where
I'll wait
   ...for Yooo Hooo!   x x x
Don't be late
     For you
     my love is true
     From
 x x   Guess Who?   x x x
P.S. my name rhymes with 'blue'

Gillian Giles scowled.

"Just look at this," she said to Katrina Kizzkurll.

"Who sent it?" asked Katrina.

"I know," said Gillian, "I know. It's from that awful Kevin Kickapoo. I'll write him a reply. Will you give it to him?"

"Okay," said tiny Katrina Kizzkurll.

Gillian took a small sheet of pink paper from her bag. It was part of a letter-writing set she'd received at Christmas. There was a little picture in the top corner of the sheet – the Three Bears, having a picnic.

To Kevin Kickapoo
 (I know it's you!)
Look,
I can't stand boys who
always shout 'HI!'
and 'YO!'
And you pick your nose!
So,
my answer is simple...
NO!
NO!
NO!

You're the worst boy in Class 2
by a million miles!
From Gillian Giles

3.00 p.m.

A Letter for N.O. Funear, Headmonster

There was no afternoon playtime in Scumbagg School. Mrs Squash, Mr Soap, and Miss Duff had to soldier on in their classrooms – without a mug of tea – until 3.30 p.m.

Headmaster Funear was luckier. At 3.00 p.m. Miss Mess took him a cup of coffee (extra strong; four sugars). She also gave him Dick Fish's two hundred lines, and an envelope.

"Ah, Dick Fish's lines," said Mr Funear.

"Yes, Headmaster," said Miss Mess.

"And an envelope."

"Yes, Headmaster," said Miss Mess.

"It says 'To N.O. Funear, Head*monster*,'" said Mr Funear in surprise.

"Yes, Headmaster," said Miss Mess.

"Please stop saying 'Yes, Headmaster' every time you speak," said Mr Funear.

"Yes, Headmaster," said Miss Mess.

The Headmaster opened the envelope. Out fell a sheet of paper. Mr Funear stared at the sheet. His mouth fell open …

"It's – it's an anonymous letter," he said at last. "An anonymous letter!"

"Yes, Headmaster," said Miss Mess.

"It's a threat!" squealed Mr Funear.

"Yes, Headmaster," said Miss Mess.

"The person who sent this must be a ... lunatic!"

"Yes, Headmaster," said Miss Mess.

"Wait a minute." Mr Funear stood up. "The Big Kipper ... The Big Kipper ... That rings a bell! I wonder ..."

Mr Funear was lost in thought.

Suddenly he said to his secretary, "You know *who* it is, don't you, Miss Mess? You know *who* sent this letter?"

"No, Headmaster," said Miss Mess.

3.30 p.m.

The End of the School Day

The school clock ticked towards half-past three. Everyone was busy clearing up. There was noise everywhere.

Mrs Squash's mob (Class 1)
   were all
      squawking
         and talking.

Mr Soap's squad (Class 2)
   were all
      hustling
         and bustling.

Miss Duff's crowd (Class 3)
   were all
      clouting
         and shouting.

There were children calling,
   children falling,
children poking,
   children joking,
children tackling,
   children cackling,
children waiting,
   children dating,
children acting really cool,
and
   children
      running
         out
            of
               school …

And everyone was waiting for,
   waiting for,
      waiting for,
         the end-of-school bell …

At precisely half-past three Miss Mess gave the school bell an extra long ring. A great cheer went up in the classrooms. Within seconds the long corridor was alive with children.

A few children stopped outside the Headmaster's room and looked at the Red Board. A new notice had been pinned up.

```
Headmaster:

N.O.Funear, BA(d)

        Scumbagg School,

        Slow Lane,

        NUTTERSALL,

        Burks. IOU 50P
```

TO THE PUPILS OF SCUMBAGG SCHOOL

Today has been a bad day.
Far too many have played the fool.

Here, to remind you, are some rules of Scumbagg School.

DON'T climb on the P.E. shed.

DON'T write silly notes.
DON'T shout in the corridor.
DON'T treat the Dinner Ladies like goats!

DON'T shout. DON'T scream.
DON'T cheek your betters.
DON'T spill paint. DON'T fight.

and

DON'T send *me* anonymous letters!

Remember,

the word you must learn is ... DON'T!

    Signed: N.O.Funear

            (Headblaster)

As usual, 'Professor' Robert R. Roberts had the last word.

"Our Headblaster," he said,
"really is a rhinoceros-sized spoilsport,
a boring big baboon,
a croaking old crow,
and the world's most wearisome windbag
... if you really want to know!"

The children gave him a round of applause. The 'Professor' bowed.

"Come on," said tiny Katrina Kizzkurll, "it's time to go home. School's over for today!"

"Three cheers!" shouted Dick Fish. And everyone bellowed,

"HOORAY!

HOORAY!

HOORAY!"

And away they all ran.
Their laughter,
 their shouts,
  their pounding feet
   faded across the playground
    and
     away
      down
       the
        s
         t
          r
           e
            e
             t